"Andrea is a masterful teacher. [The discussion guides in this book] inspire collaboration, conversation, and accountability. Her work has changed my family, and I know it will change yours too."

—**Rachel Nielson**, mother of two and podcaster at 3 in 30 Takeaways for Moms

"We've felt very strongly about limiting screens and using them wisely, but I kind of struggled with how to get everyone on board and keep them on board. We've known to be intentional. We've known to have restrictions. And we've known to protect our family from the dangers. But we were struggling with buy-in and this has helped so much!"

—**Steven** and **Sarah Harward**, parents of four

"I love having this resource—it's helping me navigate the challenges we are facing and will face [with technology in our home]. I love the research behind the information presented and the short, clear lesson [plans]. I also appreciate having ways to personalize our technology plan for our family's needs."

—**Danielle Porter**, mother of six

CREATING A TECH-HEALTHY FAMILY

10 MUST-HAVE CONVERSATIONS TO HELP YOU WORRY LESS AND CONNECT MORE WITH YOUR KIDS

ANDREA DAVIS

CREATING A TECH-HEALTHY FAMILY

For information visit: betterscreentime.com

For bulk orders or questions, contact us at: andrea@betterscreentime.com

Cover design: Jay Smith–Juicebox Designs, juiceboxdesigns.com
Interior hand-lettering and illustrations: Kristi Smith
Interior design: Emily Chambers
Editing: Sarah Monson

FAM039000   FAMILY & RELATIONSHIPS / Life Stages / School Age
FAM016000   FAMILY & RELATIONSHIPS / Education

ISBN-13: 978-1-7348859-0-3

For my husband, Tyler, my #1 team player. To my parents
and greatest cheerleaders, Bruce and Nancy, and to Elise, Eva,
Kate, Jess, and Miriam, who make the best team a mom could ask for.
Go team!

Last but not least, to you—a member of the Better Screen Time Community,
who is stepping up to parent courageously in a digital world.

CONTENTS

INTRODUCTION

On New Year's Eve 2016, our family flew across the country from Illinois to Oregon to start a new adventure. We hunkered down in temporary housing for a month while we searched for affordable housing for our family of seven. Most of our belongings and vehicles were still days behind us. Luck would have it that our new hometown was just beginning one of the harshest winters it had seen in 30 years!

In the middle of all of this, our oldest child turned 12 and was learning to navigate a new middle school. Sending a child off to school in a new place is never a fun experience. We wanted to be able to reach her, so we gave her a hand-me-down smartphone so she could contact us for things like double-checking where to get off the bus.

As time passed, we realized that while the smartphone was a great way for us to keep in touch, it was too much too soon. Because of the craziness of our lives, we hadn't taken the time to adequately prepare.

When you hand your child a smartphone, you hand them the world. And even the brightest, most responsible kids will start to lose some of their childhood because of it. It's too enticing for most kids. It will gradually take up precious time—time that could be used for making memories and learning new skills. And inevitably, it will expose them to images and ideas they are not ready for.

So we took a step back and gave our child a brick phone for over a year. We'll never regret it. During that year we talked to a lot of parents, read a lot, and started a series of family discussions with our kids. With their help, we created a family technology plan.

When you hand your child a smartphone, you hand them the world.

1

This discussion guide is the result of all of those conversations. We want to share them with you! We wish we would have had something like this to help us know where to start when teaching our children how to use technology as a tool.

HOW CAN THIS DISCUSSION GUIDE HELP YOU?

Families desperately need a strategy for how they will handle technology because there is so much at stake. Cyber bullying, pornography, inappropriate texts, anxiety, depression, and screen addictions are just a few of the issues that might affect our children, and we need a plan in place: a family technology plan!

Creating this plan is key because it will explain to your children the why behind your family's tech policies. It will be your family standard, and you'll refer to it often. It can guide you as sticky topics arise, and you'll likely make it better as time goes on.

But where should you start? One idea that helped our family is Simon Sinek's theory, Start With Why.[1] You might be familiar with Sinek's book or TED talk in which he shares how some of the world's most successful companies and leaders have inspired those around them by starting with one question: Why?

For six months our family applied this technique to the issue of how to handle technology and screen time. The result was something we called a Family Tech Think Tank, which led to a whole series of family discussions over the course of a few months on various topics relating to tech and screens.

The purpose of this guide is to help you design your own personalized family technology plan through conducting a series of Family Tech Discussions.

As our children get older, convincing them that we know what we are talking about can become difficult, but as we have meaningful

---

1 Sinek, Simon. Start with Why. Portfolio; reprint edition (December 27, 2011).

conversations, we can listen and learn together. These sessions are meant to be a foundation for ongoing conversations about technology in your home. They will also provide the groundwork necessary to develop your family technology plan.

This guide provides the framework we used for our family discussions, and it will help you get started with your own. But as with anything, it will only prove helpful if you use it. Don't delay on this one. Get started and please reach out to us with comments or suggestions. We'd love to connect!

—Andrea and Tyler

Email: andrea@betterscreentime.com
Instagram: instagram.com/betterscreentime
Facebook: facebook.com/betterscreentime

INTRODUCTION

GET READY

Brainstorm together to design a tech plan that will work for your family!

PRE-GAME WARM-UP

Before your family meets together for your first discussion, you will want to schedule some time to talk with your partner about your individual expectations regarding technology in your home.

Realize that you and your partner may not always agree—and that's okay! See it as a benefit that you may not see eye to eye on everything, because chances are your kids won't either. This conversation will help you see the situation from a new angle and allow you to process your own ideas and opinions.

If you are preparing to hold a family discussion as a single parent, spend some time thinking about current issues or potential problems your kids might have with technology and write down your ideas.

Divorced parents and/or blended families will have an additional hurdle when working with ex-spouses and children, but don't let this stop you from getting this conversation going.

The following questions and ideas will help you with your pre-game plan with your spouse:

- What is the objective or goal for your discussion with your kids? What do you hope to accomplish?

- Prepare open-ended questions to ask your children about the topic. Open-ended questions initiate dialogue and won't require a yes or no answer.

- Discuss a time limit. We found 20-30 minutes to be about right. Make your discussion as brief as possible as attention spans are limited. You can always break each portion up into more sessions if needed. You know your kids best.

- It's helpful to have a quiet activity ready for young children (pre-schoolers and younger) to do while you have the discussion with older kids.

- Make a list of specific ideas for the discussion and and jot them down in a notebook or in the blank pages within this guide.

- Decide on ground rules for a respectful discussion. This will be different for every family, depending on the ages and personalities of your children. These rules worked well for us:

  ◊ Raise your hand when you want to talk. (We have a large family.)

  ◊ Sit in a circle. (A circle is more conducive to discussion as everyone can see one another and everyone feels heard.)

- Schedule the family tech discussion on your calendar and give the kids a heads up that you will be starting a family discussion about technology to help your family be more intentional about how you use screens.

GETTING STARTED

Your goal is to inspire your family to action. You can use Sinek's Golden Circle model: "Why → How → What" as a framework for your family's discussion. We want to communicate with the innermost part of our children's brains: the limbic brain or the "feeling" part of the brain.

For example:

The "Why" is a purpose, cause or belief. Why does it matter how your family interacts with screens? Why does your family need a plan?

The "How" is what makes your family special or sets you apart. How can we use technology differently than everyone else? How can we use our devices wisely?

The "What" is basically what you do. This includes your family's rules for screen time, what apps are allowed, when kids can use devices and which ones, etc. This is often where we start by mistake! (Hey kids, this is the rule…) Then we explain "why" later when kids question the rules. Instead we want to start with "why."

We used this model as we developed this discussion series. As you follow our guide, you will go through the entire "Why → How → What" framework multiple times with your family.

SHORT ON TIME?

We understand how challenging it can be to gather everyone together for an extended period of time! You can always skip the hook (activity) section and jump right into the discussion questions. Keep this guide handy and you'll find you can have these discussions at the dinner table, in the car, or any time you have your kids' attention with minimal distractions. Just remember to take notes or record an audio memo so you can take action on what was discussed.

IT'S GAMETIME!

We've included blank pages where you can jot down your thoughts in preparation for each discussion. **Let's get started!**

FAMILY TECH DISCUSSION #1
TECHNOLOGY AS A TOOL

INTRODUCTION

Some of my favorite parenting mentors, Richard and Linda Eyre, said this about parenting in the digital age:

> *"Parents face an interesting choice. They can view the smartphone and screen time conundrum as a big, oppressive unsolvable problem, and wring their hands about it. Or they can see it as an opportunity to teach their children a wonderful form of discernment... Discernment is the skill that can help kids see both the pros and cons of technology."*[2]

Have you ever been a "hand-wringer?" I certainly have been; and some days I still am.

But guess what? You get to choose your thoughts about technology and your kids. Once I realized this, I was mentally prepared to tackle this challenge head-on and my husband Tyler jumped on board!

I can't tell you how much more confident we've become—and not because we have it all figured out. We don't. But we feel more confident about raising kids in the digital age than ever before because we've created a plan with our kids.

---

2 https://www.deseret.com/2018/2/28/20640760/don-t-force-screen-time-rules-on-your-kids-decide-on-the-rules-with-them. **Follow the Eyres on Instagram @ RichardLindaEyre.**

When I first read the quotation above, I had been tirelessly searching for ways we could better manage technology in our home. I had heard about technology plans before, and they sounded like a good idea, but all of my attempts had failed.

I still remember the night we presented our first family technology plan a few years ago. I had done all kinds of research. I talked to Tyler and made sure we were on the same page. I laid it all out to the kids: "This is how it's going to go guys!" There was a lot of squirming, blank stares, and bored faces.

Let's just say it didn't go over well. I think all the kids were wondering "What's the big deal?" and with a groan or a sigh, "More rules..." It was not a good way to get buy-in.

While there still might be some discomfort when you come up with a plan together, it's a much more meaningful and productive discussion. Plus, your kids will walk away knowing why using technology wisely even matters. I realized when I read this quote that the missing piece was involving my kids. In the past, I had dictated (in a pretty authoritative way) what would happen without including my kids in the discussion at all. I realized by involving the whole family in designing our technology plan, they would be able to learn for themselves the skill of discernment the Eyres mention.

Discernment is "the ability to judge well." It includes recognizing right from wrong and the ability to predict the consequences of one's actions. When it comes to technology, discernment can help us be the master, rather than the servant, of our devices.

As I continued to think deeply on this topic, I had a dream that left a lasting impression on me. Like most dreams, the details were a bit crazy and hard to explain. There wasn't a single screen or device in the dream, but when I woke up, the images and feelings led me to one singular message: tools can be used for bad or good, but when used improperly, the results are detrimental.

After this experience, I knew the first thing we needed to discuss with our kids was how to properly use personal devices and computers as tools. This became the foundation for all other conversations we would have about technology use in our home.

In this discussion, you will talk about the pros and cons of technology and of devices. The goal is to help your kids see technology as a tool that can help or hinder their personal progress.

MATERIALS NEEDED

- Distraction-free place

- Giant easel paper pad (or white board). We like the giant Post-it notes because they can't get erased and it's easier to transfer the notes to the computer or a piece of paper. Notes get erased more easily on a whiteboard.

- Markers. We love colored Sharpies, but if you have lots of young kids, you'll probably prefer washable markers.

If this is your first family tech discussion, make the expectations clear so the conversation is respectful and productive. We assign a scribe (always one of the kids) and take turns being the scribe each time we hold a discussion.

HOOK

We set a cell phone inside a toolbox and set the toolbox on the floor. The kids were all very curious about the toolbox! We asked, "What do you think is inside of here?" Of course, the kids answered, "tools" along with the names of tools they thought would be inside. We then asked one of the kids to open the toolbox to see what was inside. As our son opened the toolbox, he saw a hammer, screwdriver, nails, and...a cell phone. The kids looked at us puzzled. What was a cell phone doing in there? This led to our discussion questions.

DISCUSSION QUESTIONS

Here are a few questions you could ask to get the conversation started.

- How is a personal device like a tool?

- Why do you use technology?

- What do you like to do on a computer, tablet, or cell phone?

- Can tools be used improperly (or in the wrong way)?

- What are some negative or bad things we need to watch out for?

- Is there anything that you worry about when using technology?

- How can we use technology as a tool that helps us?

As your children provide answers, use your paper pad or poster to make a "thumbs up" and "thumbs down" list of the pros and cons of technology/devices. Listen and let them talk. If the conversation starts to drift, then guide the discussion back to the topic.

When you feel like you have a solid list on your poster paper, then you can ask a yes or no question: "Do you feel it's worth dealing with the "thumbs down" list in order to experience the thumbs up list?" I'm guessing your kids will say, "yes."

In that case, you can return to the why by explaining, "This is why we need to have several discussions, so that our family can use technology responsibly and try to avoid the things we listed on our thumbs down list. Over the next few weeks we will talk about using technology in more detail and come up with a technology plan for our family. We want to be able to use technology as a tool that helps us."

On the next page, you'll see an example of what our poster looked like when we were finished.

CLOCK	PORNOGRAPHY
CALCULATOR	BAD PICTURES
RESEARCH	SCAMS
MAPS	WASTING TIME
GUIDE	BAD LANGUAGE
CALL	BAD MUSIC
MESSAGE	FEELINGS OF INADEQUACY
CALENDAR	VIOLENCE/VIDEO FOOTAGE
WEATHER	CYBER BULLYING/STALKERS
MUSIC	FOMO
CHURCH TOOLS	LOSS OF SOCIAL SKILLS
NOTES	LOSS OF PHYSICAL ACTIVITY
ALARM	BAD PHONE CALLS
REMINDERS	WASTING MONEY
PICTURE/VIDEO	LOSS OF OPPORTUNITY/
TIMER	EDUCATION
GAMES	ADDICTION
SHOWS/MOVIES	FAMILY DISTRESS
EDUCATION	
SHOPPING	
GOOGLE DOCS	
HOMEWORK	
NEWS	
SOCIAL MEDIA	
VIRTUAL ASSISTANT	

Yours may look similar or totally different! The results of your Family Tech Discussion will be unique to your family. This is one of the things we love most about this idea! Each family's results and approach to using technology might be totally different. The key is that, as parents, we are being intentional and helping our children understand why it's important to prepare and plan for how we use technology.

WRAP-UP

Leave five minutes to conclude the discussion and create an action plan together. What will your family do differently because of this discussion? Pick one or two small goals or changes to make so you don't feel overwhelmed. This will also help your kids not feel like they are being attacked or forced into something they don't want to do.

"Am I using technology as a tool or is technology using me?"

As we concluded this first discussion, we decided our next actions would be to be more self-aware about how we are using technology. We decided we would ask ourselves, "Am I using technology as a tool or is technology using me?"

NEXT ACTIONS

The first step to changing human behavior is recognizing the need to change. With this in mind, we focused on self-awareness as a next action. While this may seem like a very abstract goal, this is a good place to start. Don't worry—you will start taking action in the next lesson. This is a great warm-up session before you make any big changes.

ASSESSMENT

How did it go? This is the conversation that happens after your discussion. Talk to your partner about how it went and with kids one-on-one when the opportunity comes up. We've found that when we are alone with them, our kids will sometimes bring up concerns or thoughts that they don't bring up when we are all together.

Take time to have small conversations that might help shape your future family tech discussions. You might learn it needs to be a little more relaxed and decide to have it around the kitchen table with some ice cream, or maybe someone needs more opportunities to be heard. You will figure this out as you go and make adjustments as needed.

FOLLOW-UP

This will look different for every family! For us, we tried to keep the conversation going throughout the week and address concerns as they came up.

An important element of the follow-up is to leave a visual reminder of your commitment for everyone to see. We left our poster out for a few days to remind our kids of our discussion. You could also write a simple phrase or a few bullet points from your discussion on a piece of paper and post it on the refrigerator. Bonus points if you include a silly drawing or joke that makes everyone smile when they see it!

They key here is to not drop the dialogue completely once your discussion is over. Keep the conversation going little by little.

YOU DID IT!

Now, pat yourself on the back. You've initiated your very first Family Tech Discussion! This conversation may have been easy (yet chaotic), if you have younger kids, and perhaps a bit more challenging if you have pre-teens or teens. We did this with both ages, so we get it!

As we've been studying the effects of technology on families and on individuals, we keep coming back to this quote by Dr. Laura Kastner and Dr. Jennifer Wyatt from their book, *Getting to Calm, Cool-Headed Strategies for Parenting Tweens + Teens.*[3]

"Mobile media devices are omnipresent, and the impacts on all of us are both more highly scrutinized and hotly debated. Without question, media use has significant upsides, and it is also a powerful source of reward with addictive qualities. Families struggle to find ways to enjoy the benefits, resist the harms and protect family life from excess consumption. Some speculate that the new digital divide may be between families that give in to media use to the extent that it threatens their health and relationships and other families that manage use effectively. In these families, children receive the nourishment needed from optimal sleep, stay on homework, and engage in activities and face-to-face relationships without media."

Our goal at Better Screen Time is to help you and your family be a part of the latter group. So keep the conversation going. It will be worth it!

---

3 Kaster, Laura S. and Jennifer Wyatt. *Getting to Calm: Cool-Headed Strategies for Parenting Tweens + Teens*. Parent Map, 2018.

FAMILY TECH DISCUSSION #2
FORMING A FAMILY TECHNOLOGY PLAN

INTRODUCTION

Several years ago I began working from home after being a stay-at-home mom for years. As my husband changed jobs and we moved across the country, I found myself working three different work-from-home jobs so we could continue to save money through the bumpy transition.

None of my jobs required a certain number of hours, but I had deadlines and scheduled calls at odd hours. I often found myself in our bedroom on my laptop late into the night.

After months of this, I realized this wasn't a healthy habit. It was hindering my sleep, my posture, my marriage, and my sanity. I also knew I wasn't modeling the kind of behavior I wanted to see when my future teens would have devices of their own. Something had to change.

I realized how important it was to create tech-free spaces in our home so our bedrooms could be a sanctuary for each of us. I needed to "be the change I wanted to see."

As I began to change my poor tech habits, I felt different within a week. Keeping my portable devices out of the bedrooms and bathrooms was life-changing. It motivated me even more to make a plan with our kids about where we would use screens, when we would use them, and what we were going to do on them.

I needed to "be the change I wanted to see."

In the first discussion, your family talked about *why* and *how* you use screens. Now it's time to develop a family technology plan that details the *where*, *when*, and *what* of screen use for your family. With this in mind, you can also create an approved list of sites or apps to use.

Remember your family technology plan is a work in progress, and you don't need to know *all* of the details of where, when, and what by the end of this discussion. Some ideas will come to you as you experiment and try out different strategies over the course of a few months.

Also, if you have older children or teens, this lesson may be more complicated than the first discussion. Remember to remain calm, keep things in perspective, and always try to listen. If anyone starts to become irrational or lose their temper, commit to come back to the discussion another day when everyone is ready to find a solution together. Remind everyone that the ability to speak respectfully and calmly is a sign of emotional maturity, which leads to the privilege of someday owning a personal device. (You'll talk more about this in Discussion #4.)

MATERIALS NEEDED

- Distraction-free place

- Giant easel paper pad or white board

- Markers

- Building blocks or small sticky notes

- The activity instructions (printed out for easy access)

Make the expectations clear so the discussion is respectful and productive. We assign one of the kids to be a scribe and rotate who is scribe each time we hold a Family Tech Discussion.

HOOK

Divide your kids into teams. If you have two kids or fewer, you can have the parents join the teams (even though at least one parent will know ahead of time what is going on!). Give each group some building blocks (or sticky notes) and a set of instructions, which are included as the last two pages of this discussion. (You can print these out by going to better-screentime.com/resources.)

Each group will need to build or create a building (or pattern). And each will have a different set of instructions, but don't tell them that. Give them each one minute to complete the task.

Once they are finished, compare the finished products. Then ask, "Was it easy or difficult? Why?" Have the groups compare instructions and talk about the differences. Here are some ideas that might come up:

- One group had specific instructions, and they knew what the expectations were.

- The group with the best instructions were set up for success. They knew what to do.

- Because the other team had to guess what they were supposed to do, their building/pattern didn't turn out.

Then lead into your discussion questions, starting with something like, "Why is it important to have a plan?"

DISCUSSION QUESTIONS

- Here are a few questions you could ask to get the conversation started. Keep it simple and don't feel you have to cover all of these questions.

- Why is it important to have a plan? How does having a plan help us?

- How can we apply this idea to technology and screen time?

19

- Why might it be important to have a Family Technology Plan? (We need a plan in place so we can stay safe online, avoid bad habits, protect our growing brains, and improve our relationships.)

- How can we create healthy boundaries with technology so we make sure we use it as a tool?

WHERE:

- Where in our house should we use our devices? (Keeping in mind that the things on our "thumbs down" list are more likely to occur if we are alone and bored.)

- What will our rules be for when we are in the car? (Short distances vs. long road trips.)

- What about at school, friends' homes, or other public places?

Personal examples will always have more of a lasting impact on your kids than any study ever will.

WHEN:

- What are some times of day we should focus on each other and put our devices away?

- Are there certain days or weeks when we could take a break from technology and focus on each other or friends and extended family?

- How about times of the year?

WHAT:

- What are some of your favorite places to visit online or games you like to play? (Make a list of websites and apps together, filtering through things that might fall onto the "thumbs down" list.)

- What are other great ways to use our devices that will really benefit ourselves and others?

HOW LONG:

- How much screen time does it take before we start to feel irritable or grumpy?

- How much time should we spend on a device when we are consuming?

- How much time is reasonable if we are creating something?

- What should a positive consequence be if we get off of our device when the timer goes off?

- What is a negative consequence if we don't get off when we are supposed to?

- What do we miss out on if we are on a screen for too long?

WRAP-UP

One parent can share an example from their life when they realized that a boundary or a plan they had put in place kept them safe or helped them to prioritize family, friends, or health over using a device.

For example, I let my kids know I noticed that when I stopped plugging in my phone by my bed, I went to bed earlier and slept better. The result is a well-rested mom who has more energy for her family and work. What personal examples do you have that you could share with your kids? Personal examples will always have more of a lasting impact on your kids than any study ever will.

Leave five minutes to conclude the discussion and create an action plan together. What will your family do differently because of this discussion? Pick one or two small goals or changes to make so you don't feel overwhelmed. As you work together as a family, your kids and teens will learn that they are part of the solution!

As we concluded this second discussion, we decided our goals would be:

- Avoid screens as much as possible for driving around town and short distances. Keep devices in the front console. Enjoy movies together occasionally on long road trips.

- Commit as a group to keep devices out of bedrooms (minus one phone that is plugged in right before bed in mom and dad's room for emergencies and an alarm).

- Limit screen use one day a week. For us, this is Sunday. We made a list of good uses of tech on Sunday such as FaceTime with Grandma and Grandpa.

- Take a break from tech and social media (only mom at this point) during family vacations and often during the summer.

- Politely remind friends of the no-screens-in-bedrooms rule if needed and invite them to charge their device at the charging station.

NEXT ACTION(S)

- Make a tentative Family Tech Plan (an example template is found at the end of this lesson) and post somewhere where all family members can see.

- Research and purchase a family charging station where we can leave devices in a main area in the house.

- Practice coming home from school/work and putting our phones in the charging stations rather than in our pockets. (Role-play!)

- Make a list of approved sites to visit and post by the charging station.

ASSESSMENT

Even when older children and teens don't see eye to eye with you, it's much easier to have this conversation when you're prepared and able to establish expectations. If the conversation gets a little tense, then talk to your partner about how to avoid this in the future.

FOLLOW-UP

This will look different for every family! For us, we tried to keep the conversation going throughout the week and address concerns as they came up.

An important element of the follow-up is to leave a visual reminder of your commitment for everyone to see. We wrote down the basic ideas of our tentative plan and put it on the fridge.

You'll want to assign someone in the family (it might be a parent), to transfer your plan ideas to a piece of paper or digital document.

Then we start testing it out. Remind everyone that it is a work in progress and you will make adjustments to the plan as needed.

It was after this discussion that we decided to downgrade our daughter's smartphone to a flip phone and also quit using screens in the bedrooms and the bathrooms. We had implemented this before, but it seemed a device ended up making it to the bedroom once in a while to make a video or FaceTime. I'm happy to say that after a month or so, the kids realized that this guideline was here to stay and parents were abiding by the rule, too!

GROUP A

Make this shape with your Legos or Post-It notes.

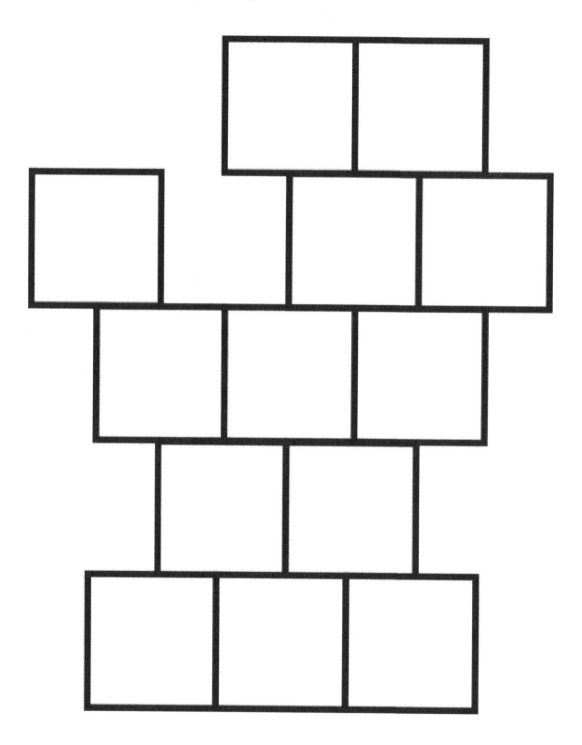

GROUP B

Make this shape with your Legos or Post-It notes.

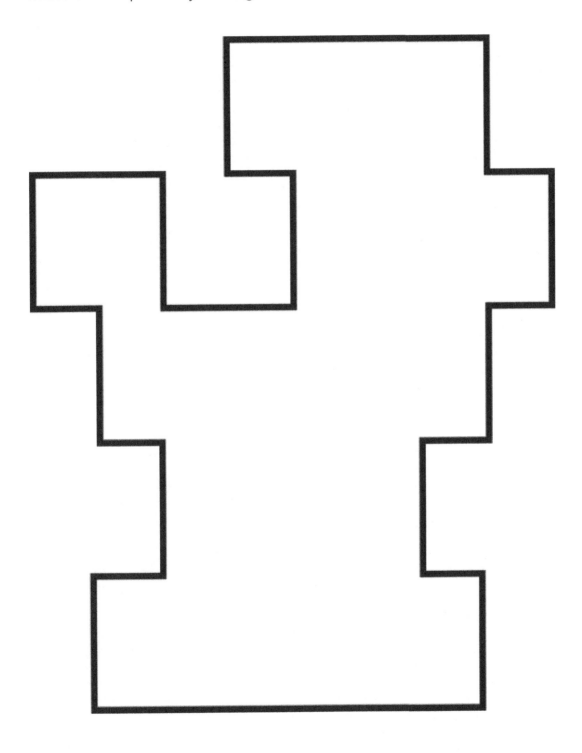

FAMILY TECHNOLOGY PLAN

WHERE?

-
-
-
-
-

WHEN?

-
-
-
-

WHAT?

-
-

HOW LONG?

-
-

ACTION ITEMS

-
-

FAMILY TECH DISCUSSION #3
HOW CAN RULES KEEP US SAFE?

INTRODUCTION

Now that you've developed a basic family tech plan, it's time to talk about the consequences for not following the plan. When we had this discussion with our family, we likened rules for screens to rules for driving a car. If we want the privilege of owning and using a personal device, then we must follow certain guidelines. The rules of the road keep us and others safe, and our family tech rules can do the same.

We wrote "R" for rule and "C" for consequence at the top of our poster. Then, we listed each of our family tech rules and came up with a consequence for not following those rules.

The first time we had this discussion, we created a consequence for every rule that was broken. We found that even with a chart, this was way too complicated! Especially for the parents. The next time we had the discussion, we let the kids come up with one *single* consequence for not following basic tech rules. They decided they wanted to do someone else's job if they broke the rule. We experimented with this for awhile, and it didn't really work. We decided on a more appropriate consequence would be to lose the privilege of using a device for the week. So far, this has been much more effective!

Please keep in mind that the kind of rules broken in our home at this stage of parenting have minimal consequences. As kids get older, the choices and the consequences can become more serious. This requires that we communicate often with each other as parents and with the child who is not following the family's tech plan. You will have to take each situation on a case-by-case basis and decide what an appropriate consequence is for the child, remembering that the child will likely need a lot of additional love, too. (Not easy!)

We also love the idea of using positive reinforcement and included rewards in our plan as well. One that works well for our younger kids is to have a planned activity with a parent when they are done using a screen. For example, before I let my son play on the computer, we might decide together that when he's finished we'll go jump on the trampoline. Then when his time is up, it's much easier for him to get off the computer, knowing we have a fun activity planned together.

> **We also love the idea of using positive reinforcement and included rewards in our plan as well.**

We reward our teenager for spending time on developing talents or doing extra work. For example, our teen is a great artist, so we've hired her several times to do graphic design for our social media channel. She was using a screen, but she was creating, not consuming. Plus, it gave us a reason to work together as a team!

You can work with your teenager to come up with some reasonable rewards that will motivate them to develop a skill or anything else that your family values over screen time.

MATERIALS NEEDED

- Distraction-free place
- Giant easel paper pad or white board
- Markers

> **It's our job as parents to teach and set limits based on information and inspiration we've received.**

Make the expectations clear so the discussion is respectful and productive. We assign one of the kids to be a scribe and rotate who is scribe each time we hold a discussion.

HOOK

Here are a few ideas you can choose from depending on the ages of your kids and the number of children:

- Have one child draw a stoplight. Let the other kids take turns coloring in the red, yellow, and green circles. Then ask, "What is this?" "What is it for?"

- Act out a scenario with toy cars where one car isn't following the traffic laws. (You could take one or two children aside ahead of time and decide who will obey and who will not obey with their toy car during the lesson. You could also role play this just as two people driving pretend cars.) Then ask, "What happened to the person who wasn't following the rules of the road?"

- For older children and teens, you can simply talk about what needs to happen before you can get a driver's license. Then ask, "Why do we need to be instructed or trained before we drive a car?"

Hopefully you'll get some responses about how rules keep us safe. They protect us and other drivers. It prevents chaos and traffic jams. Then lead into your discussion questions.

DISCUSSION QUESTIONS

Here are a few questions you could ask to get the conversation started. Keep it simple and don't feel you have to cover all of these questions.

- Why is it important to follow rules or guidelines?

- How do we benefit when we follow the rules? What good things do we experience when we follow the rules?

- Can you think of a time when you followed a rule and you were kept safe or rewarded?

- What would life be like without any rules?

- How is driving a car similar to using technology or devices?

- While we may not be in as much physical danger on a device compared to driving a car, our minds and our inner values can be harmed if we are not careful. What rules or guidelines can help us stay safe while using the internet, social media, or video games?

Try to keep your list of rules or guidelines to a bare minimum. The fewer rules there are, the better! We tried to stick with the rules that we felt had the most impact. And as much as possible, we tried to phrase the rules in positive terms.

Once you're come up with a few positively-phrased rules, now it's time to discuss consequences:

- What do you think the consequence should be for breaking one of these rules?

- What consequences would help you to keep our family's rules?

- What motivates you to do better? Consequences or rewards?

- What are some possible rewards we could try out?

Make a list of possible consequences together and let your kids know that they are just ideas! You are not committed to any of them just yet. It's an experiment.

Here are some examples of how you could rephrase "Don't" and "No" rules into positive statements:

Negatively Phrased Rules	Positive Alternatives
No screens in the bedrooms or bathrooms.	Use devices in shared family spaces.
No using screens during meals or during family time.	Let's use meal time and family activities as a time to connect with one another.
No unauthorized use.	Ask for permission to use a device or computer.
Put device in charging station when you get home.	Take a break from your device while it charges when you are home.
Get off devices and computers when asked.	Move onto a new activity when your screen time is finished.

We also love the idea of creating rewards for our kids and teens. They are usually low-budget items or activities that promote connection and fun within our family. Have fun with this and see if you can come up with a list of inexpensive, fun rewards for sticking to your family's technology plan.

WRAP-UP

Leave five minutes to conclude the discussion and create an action plan together. What will your family do differently because of this discussion? Pick one or two small goals or changes to make so you don't feel overwhelmed. As you work together as a family, your kids and teens will learn that they are part of the solution!

NEXT ACTION(S)

As we concluded this third discussion, we decided our next actions would be:

- One parent and one child would type up the list of rules and consequences and post it for the rest of the family to see. The chart would have everyone's name on it with a section to mark an "X" for a screen time infraction.

- Since that first discussion, we simplified the chart and are trying out one simple consequence for not following the rule: if someone doesn't follow the plan, they lose access to any devices for one week. We've also included some positive rewards for following the rules.

ASSESSMENT

It's always a good idea to bring up these topics again during the week while they are fresh on everyone's minds. You can use this time to assess each child's understanding and resolve any concerns. I'm learning that it is best to start the conversation by mentioning an article I read or a personal experience about how my life was enriched by following the rule. This seems to work much better than badgering kids with questions.

And if the consequences quit working after awhile, it doesn't mean you've failed—it just means your family has changed and it's time to try something new.

FOLLOW-UP

Experiment with the consequences you create and don't be afraid to abandon what doesn't work. Keep thinking and working with your children to try new ideas. Through trial and error, you will land on something that works! And if it quits working after awhile, it doesn't mean you've failed—it just means your family has changed and it's time to try something new.

FAMILY TECH DISCUSSION #4
AM I READY?

INTRODUCTION

As the parents of five children, we know each child is different. They each have different abilities, strengths, and interests. And all of these factors can affect how a child or teen interacts with an electronic device. Some kids can use a device for a while and easily walk away, while others seem to become very *attached*. Children also respond differently to discipline and rules.

Because of this, I struggled with the idea that my children would all be ready at the same time for a device of their own. I knew I couldn't just pick an age and expect that each of our children would be ready and able to handle that responsibility.

We had been a low-tech family for many years. I wanted to delay handing over a device as long as possible, yet I knew I wanted my kids to understand why and not just say "No."

As I studied and pondered this dilemma, I knew I needed to get the kids involved in the discussion. I wanted to know how to confidently answer the question, "Mom, can I have a cell phone?" with *their* solutions.

Tyler and I talked and decided we would ask the kids two simple questions to get their ideas. It turns out, our kids had some really great answers.

OBJECTIVE

In this strategy session, your family is going to create a list of indicators that will help your children know when they might be ready for a personal device. This could be a cell phone, an e-reader, or any kind of device they plan to use as their own.

33

If you have younger children and you are not even thinking of personal devices yet, you can use this discussion to talk about what responsibility is and looks like. You don't even need to talk about devices yet. I promise it will serve you well down the road—you will blink and it will be time to start talking about cell phones. You will be ahead of the game!

MATERIALS NEEDED

- Distraction-free place

- Giant easel paper pad or white board

- Markers

Make the expectations clear so the discussion is respectful and productive. We assign one of the kids to be a scribe and rotate who is scribe each time we hold a discussion.

HOOK

Have a quick relay race. Divide into two teams—parents play too! If you have teenagers and you are groaning right now, I challenge you to give this a try. Our kids are never too old for play—really!

Here are a few ideas you can choose from. Be sure to mark a starting and an ending point with some masking tape or an object. Each team will form a separate line.

Before you start, emphasize the importance of being ready for when the person in front of you returns.

Relays that work best outdoors:

- Balance an egg on a spoon! Pass the egg and spoon to the next player.

- Leap frog race. One person leapfrogs over the other.

- Crab race. Walk on hands and feet, while bent backwards.

- Wheelbarrow race. One person holds the other person's legs.

- Three-legged race using a dish towel to tie legs together.

Relays that work indoors:

- Pass an item to each other such as a pen or a lego. Whatever you have on hand! One item for each team.

- Balance a ping pong ball on a paper plate while walking and not dropping the ball.

- Shoe-box slide. Two shoeboxes for each team. Players have to shuffle/slide across the floor with one foot in each shoebox.

- Drop the penny. Put a pile of pennies into a bowl. Each team player has to pick up a penny and take it to the other side and drop it from standing height into the cup of an egg-carton (lid off).

These kinds of activities bond your family, get everyone laughing, and make something that could be really boring into something much more fun.

You can then lead into your discussion questions by asking: How did it help you to be ready when the person in front of you came back? What does it mean to be ready for something?

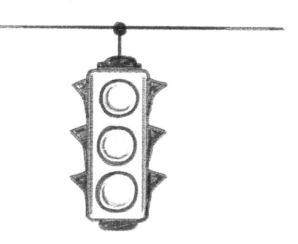

DISCUSSION QUESTIONS

Here are a few questions you could ask to get the conversation started. As your children respond, have your scribe make a list of ideas on your poster board or whiteboard. We started this conversation by asking:

- How do you know when someone is responsible? What kinds of things do they do? (Finish homework and chores, get up for school on time, brush teeth, etc.)

- What is emotional maturity? How can you tell when someone is emotionally mature? (Kind, helpful, respectful, honest, etc.)

You can then lead into questions such as:

- How can these indicators or signs help us to know when someone might be ready for a cell phone or a personal device?

- Using our list of signs of a responsible and emotionally mature person, what kinds of questions can we ask ourselves to know if we are ready or not? This question led to our final Self-Evaluation for Teens to help determine if they are ready for a device or not. This is one of our most popular downloads! You can download all twelve self-evaluation questions at betterscreentime.com/resources.

If you are already using our Self-Evaluation for Teens and it fits your family's values, that is great! Just try to let your kids have some owner-ship in this process and still have this conversation. You might decide you want to tweak a few of the questions. I strongly believe that you will know what is best for *your* family. Make this Self-Evaluation yours!

Just remember to keep the list as short as possible. We created twelve questions and felt this was as short as we could make the evaluation based on our brainstorming activity.

Also, it's very important for your kids to know that achieving 100% on this evaluation is not the goal. The goal is to be able to answer "almost always" most of the time on most of the questions. *Parents and children are learning and growing together!*

WRAP-UP

Leave five minutes to conclude the discussion and create an action plan together. What will your family do differently because of this discussion? Pick one or two small goals or changes to make so you don't feel overwhelmed. As you work together as a family, your kids and teens will learn that they are part of the solution!

NEXT ACTION(S)

As we concluded this fourth discussion, we decided our next actions would be:

- Type up our list of self-evaluation questions and post them where everyone in the family could see them. I didn't want to make getting a personal device at the forefront of everyone's attention, but for our older children it has been helpful to have this list visible when the topic comes up.

ASSESSMENT

As you experiment, you might discover that one of the questions doesn't fit your family's values, or maybe it's unreasonable due to a special family circumstance. The whole process of the Family Tech Discussion is an experiment. So, test it out, make changes if necessary, and just keep trying!

FOLLOW-UP

While our Self-Evaluation is a helpful teaching tool, my husband and I are careful to reinforce positive behavior without any mention of "earning" a device. When I see our children doing some of the things on our list, I try to compliment them and give positive feedback. I don't say anything about devices.

Similarly, when a child is repeatedly not doing something on the list, we have a talk about demonstrating emotional maturity and responsibility. Again, I don't mention the device because at the end of the day, I want them to grow into responsible adults—with or without a device.

That being said, our teenager knows and understands that by following through with the items on the Self-Evaluation that she will eventually graduate to the next "phase" in our four-phase process which you'll discuss in the next lesson!

FAMILY TECH DISCUSSION #5
THE PROGRESSION

INTRODUCTION

For most of our tech discussions, we try to let our kids provide a lot of the ideas. However, it's also our job as parents to teach and set limits based on information and inspiration we've received. These ideas can also be the basis of a family tech discussion—and this was one of those conversations for our family.

I've spent a lot of time researching and talking to other parents about the classic question: "When should I let my child have their own device?" While I wanted to delay things as long as possible, I also wanted to teach my children to use devices responsibly before they left home. I knew that smartphones were not meant for kids and felt that social media should be delayed at *least* until high school, but aside from that, I wasn't sure how to move forward. I felt paralyzed.

As I was thinking (and praying!) about this, a scripture came to my mind. Now, if you don't consider yourself to be religious in any way, hear me out on this. This concept is applicable to anyone.

The scripture teaches that we can learn "line upon line, precept upon precept. Here a little and there a little..." (Isaiah 28:10). After I thought of this scripture, the thought immediately came to my mind that we could apply this idea to screen time. We could introduce our older children to cell phones—or really any technology—through a progression or a process. Then, the following image came into my mind:

FEATURE PHONE TO SMART PHONE: A FOUR-PHASE PROCESS

BetterScreenTime

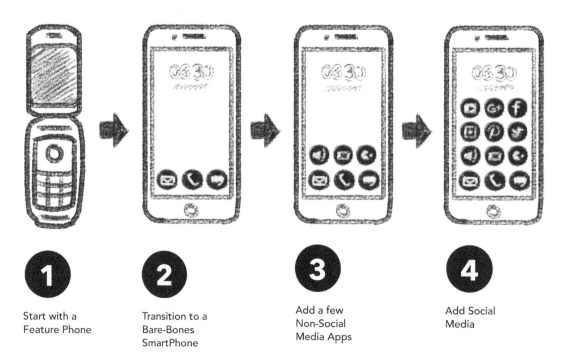

1 Start with a Feature Phone

2 Transition to a Bare-Bones SmartPhone

3 Add a few Non-Social Media Apps

4 Add Social Media

This four-phase process, combined with our Self-Evaluation for Teens, can help parents measure readiness based on the individual child rather than on a certain age. Since starting out with the process we've since adopted a smartphone without internet access as our first phone rather than a feature (brick/flip) phone. This is now an option! (You can read more about it at betterscreentime.com/resources.)

It's always a good idea to introduce things slowly.

Technology continues to change so this process might look different as time goes on. The idea is that we are not giving our children too much, too soon.

Instead, we are giving them more freedom bit by bit as they demonstrate emotional maturity and responsibility.

For the parents of younger children:

If your children are still young and not asking about a cell phone or their own device, enjoy this time and focus on modeling the kind of tech use you want to see as they grow older. They will follow your lead!

Then remember that it's always a good idea to introduce things slowly. If you need a break now and then, let them enjoy the slow-pace of older television programs and delay the touch-screens as long as you can. I promise they will catch on and figure it all out when the time is right.

MATERIALS NEEDED

- Distraction-free place

- Giant easel paper pad or white board

- Masking tape

Make the expectations clear so the discussion is respectful and productive. We assign one of the kids to be a scribe and rotate who is scribe each time we hold a tech discussion.

HOOK

Prepare for a long jump competition! Tape a long piece of masking tape to the floor. Make sure you leave yourselves plenty of room to jump.

Have everyone in the family (even the parents!) take a turn in the event. You can mark each person's landing spot with a piece of masking tape and write their initials on the tape.

This can lead into your discussion about how we are all different. We have different abilities, talents, and we are all different ages and sizes. This means that we aren't all going to be ready for the same responsibilities at the same time.

As always, feel free to adjust this activity to fit the needs of your family.

Get creative and remember—the goal is to have fun and bond as a family!

DISCUSSION QUESTIONS

Here are a few questions you could ask to get the conversation started.

Keep it simple and don't feel you have to cover all of these questions.

- Was the long jump easy or hard?

- Why did some family members jump farther than others? (We are all different. Different abilities, strengths, ages, and skills.)

- What kinds of things can babies do when they are first born?

- Why can't we feed them a hamburger when they are first born?

- How do they go from not being able to hold up their head to being able to walk a year or so later?

- What is something that used to be hard for you, but is easy for you now? (Discuss how they've practiced and progressed.)

- As we grow older, our brains become more developed and our bodies grow. We gradually learn skills to help us become independent and go out into the world on our own. We no longer rely on our parents for rides to school or activities or to pay for all of our needs. In the same way, our brains are just not ready for everything a smartphone, laptop, or tablet can do for us. They are *so* powerful! We need to learn how to use them one step at a time. How can we learn to use technology one step at at time?

- If you were a parent, how would you teach your kids to use technology step by step?

You can take notes on their answers and then introduce some ideas about a plan you might like to try with your family. It could be our four-phase process, or it could be your family's own modified version of this. You do what works best for your family!

WRAP-UP

Leave five minutes to conclude the discussion and create an action plan together. What will your family do differently because of this discussion? Pick one or two small goals or changes to make so you don't feel overwhelmed. As you work together as a family, your kids and teens will learn that they are part of the solution!

NEXT ACTION(S)

As we concluded this fifth discussion, we decided our next actions would be:

- Post the drawing of our Four-Phase Process in a visible location so everyone could become familiar with the idea.

ASSESSMENT

As your kids ask for a phone or to have more freedom, you can continue to refer to the four-phase process. Our pre-teen and teen know the process well! We continue to refer to the self-evaluation to help us determine when a teen is ready to move up to the next phase. Are they continuing to demonstrate responsibility and emotional maturity? Keep having positive conversations about what this looks like and how they can move toward being ready for the next phase. You can also use this four-phase process to work backwards if a teen has demonstrated they are not ready for the phase they are in.

FOLLOW-UP

Experiment with the process you create and don't be afraid to abandon what doesn't work. Keep thinking and work with your children to try new ideas. Through trial and error, you will land on something that works! And if it quits working after awhile, it doesn't mean you've failed, it just means your family has changed and it's time to try something new.

INTRODUCTION

One night I remember standing in the kitchen, ready to attack the pile of dirty dishes. I decided it would be more fun to open up Instagram. Just for a moment.

An hour later Tyler got home, and I realized I was still standing in the kitchen—with the pile of dirty dishes still there! Had I really spent an hour scrolling and commenting? Yes! I realized I needed to be more mindful of my social media use.

This same mind-numbing experience happens everyday to kids and adults when using social media, video games, and watching endless hours of videos. Our intentions are good: we just want to unwind for awhile. But before we know it, an hour has passed and our responsibilities still linger.

The siren song of video games, movies, and social media is a strong one. After all, they were created to be addictive. So if we allow our kids or teens to use social media, play video games, or use streaming services, we have to help them establish some boundaries.

In this discussion, your family will talk about using social media, video games, and consuming movies and online entertainment. Depending on the ages and interests of your kids, you may talk more about one than the other.

If you have teens with mixed interests, then you may need to break up this discussion into two separate conversations. You can adjust this discussion to fit your needs!

The overall theme of this conversation is to learn to be self-aware. You want your kids and teens to understand how using social media, playing video games, or watching videos might affect them personally.

We want to be the master of technology—not a slave to it—so we can create a life we love.

Share personal experiences when possible and encourage your kids to share their experiences, if they have any. Sharing your experiences will allow your kids to see your own process of learning to become self-aware with technology use.

Your older kids and teens may just roll their eyes or shrug their shoulders. That's okay. Just keep the conversation as positive as possible!

The key is to always bring the conversation back to how self-awareness can help us keep technology in its proper place in our lives. We want to be the master of technology—not a slave to it—so we can create a life we love.

MATERIALS NEEDED

- Distraction-free place

- Giant easel paper pad or white board

- Markers

- Check out our resources page at betterscreentime.com/resources for videos and articles that might help you learn more about these topics.

Make the expectations clear so the discussion is respectful and productive. We assign one of the kids to be a scribe and rotate who is scribe each time we hold a discussion.

HOOK

There are several activities you could try with your kids depending on their ages and interests. Our goal was to do an activity that creates mindfulness. Here are a few ideas:

- Do a brief yoga video together.

- Take a short walk or hike together (our favorite!).

- Play the laughing game. Each person puts their head on another person's stomach until everyone in the family is lying down in a zig-zag pattern. The first person says, "Ha." The next person, "Ha, Ha." Then the next, "Ha, Ha, Ha," and so on. The goal is to keep from laughing. Whoever laughs is out. (This person is usually me.)

- Do jumping jacks for one minute. Then have everyone put their hands on their hearts and pay attention to their heartbeats and breathing.

- Do a guided meditation for kids together. (Please see betterscreen-time.com/resources for ideas!)

DISCUSSION QUESTIONS

- Why do you think it's important to pay attention to how we're feeling?

- How do our emotions (how we feel) affect our decisions and actions?

- How can the things around us, or the activities we are doing, affect us?

- How can our activities affect our relationships with others?

Today we're going to talk about three common uses of technology. People often use them for fun, to connect with others, or to relax. However, if we don't pay attention to how they make us feel personally, they can affect how we act. What do you think these three things are?

DISCUSSION QUESTIONS–VIDEO GAMES

Here are a few questions you could ask to get the conversation started. Keep it simple and don't feel you have to cover all of these questions. We started this conversation by asking:

- What are some video games you've heard of or like to play?

- Why do some people love to play video games?

- Why do some people not like video games?

- Why do we need to be careful? What are the potential pitfalls of too much gaming?

- If we play video games in our home, what kind of games should we allow? When they are allowed? Where can they be played and with whom? How long is a reasonable amount of time?

- How do we feel if we've played video games for hours on end? Why is that?

- If it's decided we don't want to allow video games in the home, why is that? (Best to discuss it now than in the moment when a child/teen is demanding it.)

- If we play video games at friend's houses, what should we be aware of?

DISCUSSION QUESTIONS–SOCIAL MEDIA

- What is social media?

- What types of social media have you heard of or used?

- Why do people use social media?

- Why do some people choose not to use social media?

- If we choose to use social media when we are old enough, what are some personal boundaries we might create for our use?

- How can we use social media in a positive way?

- Do you think social media causes depression or anxiety in some people? Why?

DISCUSSION QUESTIONS—VIDEO STREAMING

- What kinds of movies do you like to watch?

- How do different types of movies make you feel? (Drama vs. Comedy)

- Have you noticed how YouTube, Netflix, and other streaming video services offer to play the next video for you or have a sidebar with suggestions? Why do you think that is?

- How can we be the ones to decide what we'll watch next and not leave it up to someone else (i.e. the streaming service)?

- How long should we spend "consuming" content such as YouTube or movies? How long is too long?

WRAP-UP

Leave five minutes to conclude the discussion and create an action plan together. What will your family do differently because of this discussion? Pick one or two small goals or changes to make so you don't feel overwhelmed. As you work together as a family, your kids and teens will learn that they are part of the solution!

NEXT ACTION(S)

As we concluded this sixth discussion, we decided our next actions would be:

- Keep video games at a minimum in our home, (not a lot of interest in our house).

- Mom will stick with her social media limits per day and use the Screen Time feature on her iPhone to continue to be off of devices between 9 p.m. and 7 a.m.

- Kids won't use social media until they are an advanced teen, have used their phone responsibly up to that point, and have made significant progress toward becoming more emotionally mature based on our Self-Evaluation for Kids and Teens.

Your next actions might look completely different. Your next steps should be catered to your own family based on your discussion.

Be sure to add any necessary changes to your Family Technology Plan.

ASSESSMENT

This category will likely change a lot as your kids grow older! You can have this conversation (or a variation of it) over and over again until your family comes up with a solution. Remember, you can test out your ideas, make changes if necessary, and just keep trying!

FOLLOW-UP

As parents, the most important follow-up begins with how we model our use of these tools.

As parents, the most important follow-up begins with how we model our use of these tools.

Tyler used to play video games as a teen, but hasn't played for years and doesn't use social media. I (Andrea) use social media to share our Better Screen Time message with the world. With that in mind, I use my

50

personal social media accounts less than I used to. Managing multiple social media accounts can consume a lot of time, so I have to create boundaries around how much time I will spend on social media.

Every family will be different. If you play video games, use social media or frequently watch YouTube or online videos, how could you set an even better example for your kids? It all starts with you.

FAMILY TECH DISCUSSION #7
BEING SMART AND SAFE ONLINE

INTRODUCTION

'Il never forget the day a letter arrived in the mail addressed to one of my favorite passwords. The envelope didn't even have my name on it!

I immediately felt a pit in my stomach. I was sure I had never shared my password with anyone, but in a world where passwords can and do get sold, I realized that someone could easily access my personal information.

I quickly changed my password for various accounts and realized I needed to take my online security more seriously.

I have since shared this experience with our kids. Sometimes we assume our kids know all the things we do; but that isn't always the case.

This family discussion gives you the opportunity to talk about the importance of being smart and safe when using the Internet.

Sometimes we assume our kids know all the things we do; but that isn't always the case.

MATERIALS NEEDED

- Distraction-free place

- Giant easel paper pad (or white board)

- Markers

- Check out betterscreentime.com/resources for videos and articles that might help you learn more about these topics.

Make the expectations clear so the discussion is respectful and productive. We assign one of the kids to be a scribe and rotate who is scribe each time we hold a think tank discussion.

HOOK

Memory, anyone? Our younger kids love playing a good game of Memory.

If you don't have a Memory game, you could print one out. (Just do a quick Google search for a printable Memory game.) The Dollar Store often has some, too.

If you have a large family, you could even split up into teams and run several games at the same time. Older teens might prefer a playing card version of Memory (Google it!) or even a Chess tournament.

DISCUSSION QUESTIONS

Here are a few questions you could ask to get the conversation started. Keep it simple and don't feel you have to cover all of these questions.

- How did you keep track of certain cards when playing Memory? (Remembered where they were or noticed where they fit in a pattern, remembered the image, etc.)

- Our brains are quick to recognize patterns just like in the game of Memory. They are always trying to make sense of what we see. How can we use these same brain skills to help us stay safe online? (Recognize patterns or behaviors.)

- What do we need to watch out for when we are using the Internet?

- What about when using email?

- What are some warning signs that someone is trying to get information from me?

- What is personal information and who should I share it with?

- Why are passwords important? And what should we do to keep our passwords safe? (Conversation about smart passwords and changing them.)

- What should I do if someone is being mean to me online/social media?

- How can I protect myself?

WRAP-UP

Leave five minutes to conclude the discussion and create an action plan together. What will your family do differently because of this discussion? Pick one or two small goals or changes to make so you don't feel overwhelmed. As you work together as a family, your kids and teens will learn that they are part of the solution!

NEXT ACTION(S)

As we concluded this seventh discussion, we decided our next actions would be:

- Use strong passwords.

- Never give anyone else our password, except our parents/spouse.

- Change our passwords several times per year.

- Don't share personal information with anyone we don't know or trust.

- Remember the Golden Rule in our online interactions and show kindness.

- Delete, block, ignore—and tell someone—if we feel we are being cyberbullied.

ASSESSMENT

After you have this discussion with your kids, watch for real-life examples of staying safe online. News articles, personal experiences, and conversations about what kids are learning at school about online safety are all great ways to keep the conversation going.

FOLLOW-UP

Help teens change passwords, if needed, and make sure you know their passwords.

Take a look at your Family Technology Plan to see if you need to add anything from this discussion.

FAMILY TECH DISCUSSION #8
DON'T TAKE CHANCES WITH PORNOGRAPHY

INTRODUCTION

Growing up in the 1980s and early '90s, a person usually had to go looking for pornography in order to find it. But today it is possible for kids to encounter pornography through a text message from a friend or by simply watching a YouTube video supposedly created for kids. Pornography is especially harmful to children—and it is pervasive. (Please see betterscreentime.com/resources to learn more about the dangers of pornography.)

A few years ago, I clicked on the search button on Instagram to check it out. It took less than a minute for a pornographic image to show up. I quickly clicked off the app and immediately knew I needed to do a better job at preparing my kids. It's not a question of *if* our kids will see pornography, but *when*. Children are being exposed to pornography at an earlier age than ever before. As parents, we need to help our children know what to do when they see pornography.

We have to start with educating our kids and giving them the tools they need to reject porn.

We can start with a very basic conversation when our kids are little about our bodies and what it means to respect and love our bodies. We can then later talk about respecting others' bodies and eventually about good pictures, bad pictures, and what to do if we see a bad picture.

This conversation about bodies can also lead to discussions about sex and healthy relationships. Every family will approach this subject differently, but it's crucial for us to talk about it as frequently, and as naturally as possible. Many kids and teens seek out pornography because they are curious about sex. We want our kids to turn to us with their questions first. Check out betterscreentime.com/resources if you're interested in some great books to help guide you in this conversation.

Even if we feel that we've safeguarded all of our own family and our devices, our kids and teens can easily be exposed to pornography from someone else. We have to start with educating our kids and giving them the tools they need to reject porn.

One idea we implemented in this discussion was the concept of creating your own acronym to remember how to run from porn. Our kids liked making up their own defensive plan, and I think they'll likely remember it since they created it. Your kids might love creating their own acronym as well!

One final note: you may want to have separate conversations with your kids on this topic depending on their ages and maturity.

MATERIALS NEEDED

- Distraction-free place

- Giant easel paper pad (or white board)

- Markers

- I strongly recommend these books for this discussion. We used both because we have mixed ages, but you can choose the one that best fits your age group:

  ◊ *Good Pictures Bad Pictures Jr.: A Simple Plan to Protect Young Minds* by Kristen Jenson (recommended for ages 3-6)

  ◊ *Good Pictures Bad Pictures: Porn-Proofing Today's Young Kids* by Kristen Jenson (recommended age is 8+)

  Both of these books can be found at betterscreentime.com/resources.

Make the expectations clear so the discussion is respectful and productive. We assign one of the kids to be a scribe and rotate who is scribe each time we hold a tech discussion.

HOOK

Gather the family around and read one of the *Good Pictures, Bad Pictures* books (pick the one that best fits your kids' ages). If you read the longer version, you will want to read it ahead of time and possibly summarize the main points in the book as you show the pictures. You could also just break up this discussion into multiple discussions if you want to read it word for word. It contains a lot of information. You can then lead into a family discussion centered on the ideas in the book.

DISCUSSION QUESTIONS

Here are a few questions you could ask to get the conversation started. Keep it simple and don't feel you have to cover all of these questions.

- Images and videos can bring back great memories and remind us of loved ones. They can invoke powerful feelings that go straight to our brain and make us feel a certain way. Because of this, we have to be careful about what kinds of images and videos we see. When you are using a computer or a device, we might see an image or video that startles us or shocks us because a person isn't wearing any or very little clothing. What is this called?

- When we feel shocked, what is our brain trying to tell us?

- Even if we are very careful when using the Internet, we might see pornography. How will we know if it's pornography?

- What should we do if we see pornography?

- Are we in trouble if we see a bad picture?

- Is there anything we can do to try to prevent seeing pornography again?

- Why is it important that we don't go looking for pornography? How can looking at pornography affect us and our relationships with others?

- People are wired for connection, but sometimes people who become addicted to pornography mistakenly satisfy this need for connection with images instead of with real people. How could that cause a problem?

If you use *Good Pictures Bad Pictures: Porn-Proofing Today's Young Kids* there are some great discussion questions at the end of each chapter that can help facilitate this discussion as well!

We reviewed the CAN DO™ plan in the book and worked together to memorize the steps to the plan. The CAN DO™ plan is based on science and each step is intentional and essential.

Our kids wanted to make up their own acronym based on the ideas from the CAN DO™ plan. This is completely optional, but it can be a great way for your kids to retain and own the information.

Our kids wanted to use the word WAR. (Like they are fighting a war against bad pictures!) Here is their acronym:

W = Walk away

A = Alert someone

R = Relax

It's simple, and not perfect, but it helped to solidify some of the ideas they had learned from the CAN DO™ plan. The idea is to get your kids involved so they will know what they need to do when they are first exposed to pornography and know what to do with the shocking memories that keep coming up in their minds after they are exposed.

Kristen Jenson, author of *Good Pictures Bad Pictures* has said, "For kids to thrive in the digital age, they need an internal filter that will help them reject pornography no matter where they go." Your goal with this discussion is to help build that internal filter!

Several months later, we talked about the 10-minute rule. The 10-minute rule comes from Deanna Lambson who created an Internet Safety program for schools called White Ribbon Week. The 10-minute rule means we will tell a trusted adult (parent or teacher) if we see anything that makes us feel bad or uncomfortable within ten minutes.

It's crucial for parents to start this conversation with their kids early on so they know they can talk to us when they encounter pornography.

This rule applies to parents, too! Tyler and I try to tell each other within ten minutes if we've seen anything inappropriate. We committed to the 10-minute rule as a family.

Deanna teaches, "One of the highest indicators of whether a child will return to a pornographic image is whether or not the child has told an adult." When our kids talk about what they've seen their brain is able to let it go, instead of worrying about it. It's crucial for parents to start this conversation with their kids early on so they know they can talk to us when they encounter pornography.

Deanna later stated that there is nothing magic about ten minutes! You could certainly make it a two-minute rule. The sooner the better! The best way to get rid of that shame or bad feeling, is to tell someone we trust as soon as we can.

The ten-minute rule applies to intentional as well as unintentional viewing of pornography. As parents we can model this rule and reassure our

61

children and teens in advance that even if they get curious or make a mistake, we won't get mad at them or stop loving them.

WRAP-UP

Leave five minutes to conclude the discussion and create an action plan together. What will your family do differently because of this discussion? Pick one or two small goals or changes to make so you don't feel overwhelmed. As you work together as a family, your kids and teens will learn that they are part of the solution!

NEXT ACTION(S)

As we concluded this eighth discussion, we decided our next actions would be:

- Research Internet filters in addition to the basic OpenDNS filter we were using. (See betterscreentime.com/resources to learn more about OpenDNS and other filters.)

- Keep the conversation going and read the *Good Pictures, Bad Pictures* books with the kids several times throughout the year.

Some other potential next actions could be to:

- Post your family acronym by your family computer or device as a reminder of your action plan to reject pornography.

- Make plans to act out various scenarios (of when your children could potentially encounter porn) to help your kids practice using the action plan.

- Increase your own awareness as a parent by learning more about the harmful effects of pornography. Learn more at betterscreentime.com/resources.

- If one of your children is currently viewing pornography make a plan to have regular check-ins and check betterscreentime.com/resources for additional resources on how to proceed.

ASSESSMENT

How did it go? Take time to talk with your partner about how your discussion went. You can also talk with your kids one-on-one when the opportunity comes up. We've found that our kids will sometimes bring up concerns or thoughts when we are alone with them that they don't bring up when we are all together.

FOLLOW-UP

If you don't have any Internet filters set up in your home, start looking into installing one. Ask other parents what they use and why they like it. And remember, the best filter is an internal filter. Having an on-going open dialogue about this topic will help your children and teens start to develop their own internal filter.

FAMILY TECH DISCUSSION #9
HEALTHY RECHARGING

INTRODUCTION

One day, when I was about 17, I remember telling a trusted adult about an occasional habit I turned to when I felt stressed out: "When I'm having a bad day, I go down to the corner drug store," (I know you're getting worried about me at this point, so keep reading...), "and I get a cherry Coke. They mix it up for you, and they have the best pebble ice."

As I confided my little secret, this person smiled and said, "Oh, Andrea. That's much better than what I did when I was your age and felt stressed out."

While I don't recommend sugar as a positive coping mechanism, this conversation taught me that there were better and worse things I could use to cope with the challenges of growing up. I also learned as a teenager that I needed more laughter in my life. I'm a natural worrier, and I found that I could turn to *Calvin and Hobbes* to help me to laugh. It became one of my favorite ways to unwind. It still is.

Have you talked to your kids about how you personally cope with stress? Do you try to model positive coping strategies for your kids? It can be tough! But it's critical for us to take the time to talk to our kids about how to handle stress and anxiety.

Many headlines will tell us that our phones are actually creating anxiety and depression, but the more I've researched the topic, I've learned it's a question of the chicken vs. the egg. Which came first? Do the phones create those feelings, or do we turn to our phones for comfort because we already have those feelings due to other circumstances?

I think the answer will be different for everyone. That's why it's important for us to look beyond flashy headlines and discover what's at work in our own lives.

Perhaps the more important issue is that we need to teach our children healthy ways to deal with stress and discouragement. This discussion will help you to engage in this dialogue with your family.

> **It's important for us to look beyond flashy headlines and discover what's at work in our own lives.**

MATERIALS NEEDED

- Distraction-free place

- Giant easel paper pad (or white board)

- Markers

- Check out our betterscreentime.com/resources for videos and articles that might help you learn more about these topics.

Make the expectations clear so the discussion is respectful and productive. We assign one of the kids to be a scribe and rotate who is scribe each time we hold a discussion.

HOOK

Pick a favorite family activity to do together! It might be jumping on the trampoline, playing a board game, a game of flag football, or a kitchen dance party. Just pick something that is screen-free and that will get everyone interacting and laughing. The idea is to experience a healthy, recharging activity together.

DISCUSSION QUESTIONS

Here are a few questions you could ask to get the conversation started. As your kids respond, make a list of favorite, screen-free activities or ways to unwind. Use vocabulary your kids will understand best depending on their age and maturity.

- What do you like to do for fun?

- What activities do you like to do alone? With a friend? With the family? What does healthy recharging look like? (Some people try to make themselves feel better by repeatedly using (abusing) substances or even turning to pornography, video games, or social media to try to make them feel better.)

- What do you do when you're stressed? Is there a better way to handle the stress in your life?

- How can we (parents/family members) help you out when you are feeling sad or overwhelmed? What do you like or not like?

- How will the activities on this list help us to handle stress?

WRAP-UP

Leave five minutes to conclude the discussion and create an action plan together. What will your family do differently because of this discussion? Pick one or two small goals or changes to make so you don't feel overwhelmed. As you work together as a family, your kids and teens will learn that they are part of the solution!

NEXT ACTION(S)

As we concluded this ninth discussion, we decided our next actions would be:

- Post our list of screen-free activities where we can see them.

- Next time we are bored, stressed, or sad, do one of the activities on our list.

ASSESSMENT

Continue to model healthy recharging! Some adults (me!), have to actually schedule this in. I'm not wired to take it easy, so I have to schedule a weekly hike with a friend. Many parents are juggling so many responsibilities, it can be difficult to find time to unwind.

As our kids and teens start to feel anxiety and stress creep in, we can intervene in a loving way and encourage some of the ideas on the list we created together.

Sometimes we want to take the easy route—plopping on the couch in front of a tv or our phone. I think this is completely normal and okay once in awhile. But, we have to ask ourselves, "Is this activity going to give me the results I want? Will it make me feel replenished and ready to tackle life again?"

Then as our kids and teens start to feel anxiety and stress creep in, we can intervene in a loving way and encourage some of the ideas on the list we created together. As anxiety and depression is on the rise, this is a vital skill we can teach our children in our home.

FOLLOW-UP

Keep adding to your list as you think of more activities you enjoy. Refer to it when anyone in the family needs a little lift or stress relief!

FAMILY TECH DISCUSSION #10
CRAFT A VISION

INTRODUCTION

You've made it! This is your final discussion; although we hope it won't be your last. By now, you and your kids know how to have these conversations. Some families struggle to reach this point because parents feel overwhelmed and kids feel frustrated. We know—we've been there!

Our family has cycled through several of these discussion topics more than once. Kids grow up, technology changes, and suddenly there is a new topic to discuss. The good news is that you now have a solid plan that just needs some finetuning by crafting a vision of your family's future.

This is the part where we hope our kids start to internalize personal values and make individual commitments about how they will use technology as they grow older. This is what will make these discussions stick!

You might be familiar with Stephen R. Covey's book, *The 7 Habits of Highly Effective People*. Covey encourages us to "begin with the end in mind" and "start with a clear destination." This advice has guided Tyler and me over the years as we've made important decisions for our family.

As you consider the role technology plays in your family, think about what you want your family to look like in 5 years, 10 years, and beyond. How do you want to use your devices now so technology doesn't interfere with those relationships down the road? What goals and dreams does your family have that will only be possible if you are the masters of your devices and not slaves?

Understanding *why* using technology responsibly matters and having a personal commitment will make all the difference for our families.

As you talk to your kids about your family's values, character traits, goals, and dreams, you will work together to craft a vision statement for your family. (Some call it a mission statement, philosophy, manifesto, or creed—use whatever feels natural for your family.)

The key idea is to take the most important ideas from your brainstorming session and write a brief statement describing your family's approach to technology. You can check out our family's vision statement at better-screentime.com/resources.

Creating a vision statement not only helps us to "begin with the end in mind," but to put our "big rocks" in place first, as Covey taught. When we prioritize those things that matter most, it will be easier to avoid filling our lives with the nonessential, "small rocks" that can so easily absorb our time, energy, and if we're not careful, our relationships.

As you wrap up this final discussion, you'll feel more confident in your ability to parent in the digital era and your kids will eventually be more mindful of making better choices because they will understand why it matters.

I can't wait to hear what your family comes up with! Please reach out to me and share your family's vision statement so we can inspire other families to do the same.

MATERIALS NEEDED

- Distraction-free place

- Giant easel paper pad or white board

- Large clear container

- Several big rocks and many small rocks (enough to fill your container)

- Check out betterscreentime.com/resources for videos and articles that might help you learn more about these topics.

Make the expectations clear so the discussion is respectful and productive. We assign one of the kids to be a scribe and rotate who is scribe each time we hold a discussion.

HOOK

Gather several big rocks and many small rocks.

- Ask one of the kids to put the big rocks in the container first. Ask some of the discussion questions about big rocks and then ask the other kids to all come and take a turn putting the small rocks into the container as you begin the discussion. You can also try putting the small rocks in first and see if you can fit the big rocks in! It's a great way to start this discussion.

DISCUSSION QUESTIONS

Here are a few questions you could ask to get the conversation started. Keep it simple and don't feel you have to cover all of these questions.

- What are the big rocks for our family? (Encourage your kids to think about the things that matter most/the things we don't want to live without.)

- Why should we put the big rocks in the container before the small rocks?

- What are the small rocks in our lives? (Things that are nice, but not necessary?)

- When I think of being a _____ (your family's last name), I think of… (Have your family brainstorm a list of values and character traits unique to your family.)

- What hobbies or activities does our family love?

- What are some of our family's goals and dreams?

- What does responsible tech use look like for our family?

- Why is it important that we use technology wisely?

- What will each of our lives look like if we learn to be the masters of technology and not the other way around? How will that help each of us live out our full potential?

WRAP-UP

Leave five minutes to write a family vision statement together. It doesn't need to be elaborate or well written at this point. Let it be messy, raw, and real. How do you want to use technology now so you can have strong family ties now and in the future?

NEXT ACTION(S)

As we concluded this tenth discussion, we decided our next actions would be:

- Update your Family Tech Plan and include your family's vision statement. Print and post on the fridge or a visible location.

ASSESSMENT & FOLLOW-UP

After we had finished our family discussions over the course of many months, our oldest teen graduated to phase two of our four-phase process. We scheduled a time to sit with her one-on-one to review our Family Tech Plan and our rewards and consequences. We felt this was more effective than using a cell phone contract because it holds everyone accountable. It helps teens feel more empowered and less controlled.

We later worked with her to create a pledge that included her own values. (You can learn more about how to do this in our course *Untangling Teens & Tech* by going to betterscreentime.com/resources.)

Keep the conversation going with your partner and kids to make sure your Family Technology Plan stays up to date!

You did it! We're sending you a huge high five.

FAMILY DISCUSSIONS
CONCLUSION

As our family worked through these discussions, one conversation at a time, I began to feel more confident in my ability to raise our kids in the digital era. I no longer felt panicky about the devices in our home.

Do I still worry? Definitely. But I feel prepared, not scared. I'm ready to help coach my kids through the challenges that will inevitably come.

I hope you are also feeling more confident and inspired to help your kids thrive in a digital world.

And now, I want to leave you with one last dose of inspiration.

I thought that this process of creating healthy technology boundaries through a family tech plan was just that: a means to an end. But I realized it was much more.

Through this process, *my kids have taught me*, and I've realized that even difficult conversations can bring us closer together if we are focused on the person in front of us rather than on the outcome.

Never let a problem to be solved become more important than a person to be loved.

One of my favorite bits of parenting advice is the line, "Never let a problem to be solved become more important than a person to be loved."[5] This certainly isn't easy, and it's taken a lot of practice on my part. But I've learned that when we focus on our children's needs and on loving them, the outcome will work itself out.

---

5 Barbara Johnson (see "Quotable Quotes," Reader's Digest, Jan. 1997, 161).

Your technology plan will evolve into just what it should be for *your* family. Even though you may stumble through it at times, in the process you will be connecting with your kids. By showing up imperfectly, you let your kids know that they are worth it.

At the end of the day, it is these connections with those we love that really matter. Keep showing up and connecting with what really matters—your kids!

We're here to cheer you on.

Tyler & Andrea

IDEAS AND NOTES

BetterScreenTime

*Do you want additional help managing technology with
your family? Check out our online courses by going to*

betterscreentime.com/resources

*We're here to help you worry less and
connect more with your kids!*

ABOUT THE AUTHOR

Andrea Davis is the founder of Better Screen Time. She has a B.A. in secondary education. However, her greatest learning has come from being in the (tech) trenches as a stay-at-home mom. She lives in beautiful Hood River, Oregon with her husband, Tyler, and their five children.

Made in the USA
Monee, IL
13 April 2021